Classic Cocktail Guides
and Retro Bartender Books

Oxford Night Caps

A Collection of Recipes for
Making Various Cups, Beverages,
and Cocktails Used in the University

Richard Cook

Historic Cookbooks of the World
Kalevala Books, Chicago

"I wonder anybody does anything at Oxford but dream and remember, the place is so beautiful. One almost expects the people to sing instead of speaking. It is all like an opera."
— William Butler Yeats, 1865–1939

Oxford Night Caps:
A Collection of Recipes for Making Various Cups, Beverages, and Cocktails Used in the University

Joanne Asala, Series Editor

Classic Cocktail Guides and Retro Bartender Books and *Historic Cookbooks of the World* are published by Kalevala Books, an imprint of Compass Rose Technologies, Inc. Titles published by Kalevala Books are available at special quantity discounts to use as premiums and sales promotions or for academic use. For more information, please e-mail us at editor@compassrose.com or write to:

Compass Rose Technologies, Inc.
PO Box 409095
Chicago, IL 60640

Editors' Note

Some ingredients found in vintage cocktail guides are unavailable or hard to come by today. Check out our resource guide at the back for vendors who specialize in hard-to-find ingredients and websites with information on how to recreate classic cocktails and cocktail ingredients.

ISBN: 978-1-880954-38-6

OXFORD

Night Caps.

A

COLLECTION OF RECEIPTS

FOR MAKING

VARIOUS BEVERAGES

USED IN

THE UNIVERSITY.

A NEW EDITION, ENLARGED.

OXFORD:

SLATTER & ROSE, 2 & 3, HIGH STREET.

MDCCCLXXI.

OXFORD

𝕹𝖎𝖌𝖍𝖙 𝕮𝖆𝖕𝖘.

A

COLLECTION OF RECEIPTS

FOR MAKING

VARIOUS BEVERAGES

USED IN

THE UNIVERSITY.

Quid non ebrietas designat ? Operta recludit,
Spes jubet esse ratas, ad prœlia trudit inertem,
Sollicitis animis onus eximit, addocet artes.
Fecundi calices quem non fecere disertum ?
Contracta quem non in paupertate solutum ?
Hor. lib. i, ep. 5.

What cannot wine perform ? It brings to light
The secret soul ; it bids the coward fight ;
Gives being to our hopes, and from our hearts
Drives the dull sorrow and inspires new arts,
Whom hath not an inspiring bumper taught
A flow of words and loftiness of thought !
Even in th' oppressive grasp of poverty
It can enlarge, and bid the wretch be free.
Francis.

A NEW EDITION, ENLARGED.

OXFORD,
SLATTER & ROSE; 2 & 3, HIGH STREET.
MDCCCLXXI.

Historic Cookbooks of the World

CONTENTS.

Historic Cookbooks of the World

Classic Cocktail Guides and Retro Bartender Books

NIGHT CAPS.

BISHOP, OR SPICED WINE.

Three cups of this a prudent man may take;
The first of these for constitution's sake,
The second to the girl he loves the best,
The third and last to lull him to his rest.

Ancient Fragment.

BISHOP seems to be one of the oldest winter beverages known, and is to this day preferred to every other, not only by the *youthful votary of Bacchus* at his evening's revelry, but also by the *grave Don* by way of a Night Cap; and probably derives its name from the circumstance of ancient dignitaries of the Church, when they honoured the University with a visit, being regaled with spiced wine. It appears from a work published some years since, and entitled, *Oxoniana, or Anecdotes of the University of Oxford*, that in the Rolls or

B

Accounts of some Colleges of ancient foundation, a sum of money is frequently met with charged "*pro speciebus*," that is, for spices used in their entertainments ; for in those days as well as the present, spiced wine was a very fashionable beverage. In the Computus of Maxtoke Priory, anno 1447, is the following curious entry : " Item pro vino cretico cum speciebus et confectis datis diversis generosis in die Sancti Dionysii quando *Le fole* domini Montfordes erat hic, et faceret jocositates suas in camera Orioli," " *Vinum creticum* " is supposed to be raisin wine, or wine made of dried grapes ; and the meaning of the whole seems to be this : Paid for raisin wine with comfits and spices, when Sir S. Montfort's fool was here, and exhibited his merriments in the Oriel chamber.

Recipe.

Make several incisions in the rind of a lemon, stick cloves in the incisions, and roast the lemon by a slow fire. Put small

but equal quantities of cinnamon, cloves,
mace and all-spice, into a saucepan with
half a pint of water ; let it boil until it is
reduced one half.   Boil one bottle of port
wine ; burn a portion of the spirit out of
it, by applying a lighted paper to the
saucepan.   Put the roasted lemon and spice
into the wine ; stir it up well, and let it
stand near the fire ten minutes.   Rub a
few knobs of sugar on the rind of a lemon,
put the sugar into a bowl or jug, with
the juice of half a lemon, (not roasted,)
pour the wine into it, grate some nutmeg
into it, sweeten it to your taste, and serve
it up with the lemon and spice floating in it.

Oranges, although not used in Bishop at
Oxford, are, as will appear by the following
lines, written by Swift, sometimes introduced
into that beverage.

Fine oranges
Well roasted, with sugar and wine in a cup
They'll make a sweet Bishop when gentlefolks sup.

LAWN SLEEVES, CARDINAL,
AND POPE,

Owe their origin to some Brazenose Bac-
chanalians, and differ only from Bishop as
the species from the genus.

LAWN SLEEVES,

Substitute madeira or sherry for port
wine, and add three glasses of hot calves-
feet jelly.

CARDINAL.

Substitute claret for port wine ; in other
respects the same as Bishop.

POPE.

Precisely the same as Bishop, with the
exception of champagne being used instead
of port wine.

CIDER BISHOP.

Omit the wine, and add one bottle of good cider, a quarter of a pint of brandy and two glasses of calves-feet jelly in a liquid state.

OXFORD MULL.

Boil a small quantity of cinnamon, cloves, and mace in half a pint of water; pour into it one bottle of port wine, and when it is nearly boiling, add two lemons thinly sliced. Sweeten it to your taste, and it is fit for use.

NEGUS.

Negus is a modern beverage, and, according to Malone, derives its name from its inventor, Colonel Negus. Dr. Willich, in his "Lectures on Diet and Regimen," says, that Negus is one of the most innocent and wholesome species of drink; especially if Seville oranges be added to red port wine, instead of lemons; and drunk moderately, it possesses considerable virtues in strengthening the stomach; but, on account of the volatile and heating oil in the orange peel, Negus, if taken in great quantities, is more stimulant and drying than pure wine.

WHITE WINE NEGUS.

Extract the juice from the peeling of one lemon, by rubbing loaf sugar on it; or cut the peeling of a lemon extremely thin, and pound it in a mortar. Cut two lemons into thin slices; four glasses of calves-feet jelley in a liquid state; small quantities of cinnamon, mace, cloves, and all-spice. Put the whole into a jug, pour one quart of boiling water upon it, cover the jug close, let it stand a quarter of an hour, and then add one bottle of boiling hot white wine. Grate half a nutmeg into it, stir it well together, sweeten it to your taste, and it is fit for use.

Seville oranges are not generally used at Oxford in making Negus; when they are, one orange is allowed to each bottle of wine.

COLD WHITE WINE NEGUS.

To make white wine Negus, let the mixture stand until it is quite cold, and then pour a bottle of white wine into it.

It is sometimes in the summer season placed in a tub of ice: when that is done it will be necessary to make the Negus somewhat sweeter, as extreme cold detracts from the sweetness of liquors.

PORT WINE NEGUS.

In making port wine Negus, merely omit the jelly: for when port wine comes in contact with calves-feet jelly, it immediately assumes a disagreeable muddy appearance.

Negus is not confined to any particular sorts of wine; if the jelly is omitted, it can be made with any, or several sorts mixed together.

SHERRY COBBLER.

Sherry Cobbler has only been recently introduced into the University, and has become a great favourite among the Undergraduates. It unfortunately happened, that on its first introduction, ice was procured from the Confectioners and Fishmongers which had been taken from stagnant ponds and noisome ditches; consequently those who partook of it imbibed the filthy impurities which it contained. Subsequently the lemon, grape, strawberry, and other pure and wholesome water ices of the Confectioners, have been substituted.*

Recipe.

Pound a small quantity of ice quite fine, by wrapping it in a coarse cloth, and beating it with a mallet or rolling pin. Half fill a large tumbler with this powdered ice, add a teaspoonful and a half of pounded

* This liquor, drawn into the mouth through a straw, has in more than one instance produced Vertigo.

sugar, two or three pieces of the outer rind of a lemon, and a wine glass and a half of sherry. (Throw in half a dozen strawberries, if in season.) Fill up with pounded ice. Mix by pouring rapidly from one tumbler to another several times. Drink through a straw.

This fashionable compound was published by a party of speculating gentlemen, who have denominated themselves "the Wenham Lake Ice Company." And it appears, that the Company imports an immense quantity of ice from Wenham lake in America, which is transmitted to any part of the united kingdom by American refrigerators or portable ice houses, and sold through the agencies of Tradesmen residing at Liverpool, Birmingham, Manchester, Dublin, Hastings, Richmond, and Blackheath.

———

JULAP, OR JULEP.

Behold this cordial *Julap* here,
That flames and dances in his crystal bounds,
With spirits of balm and fragrant syrups mixt:
Milton.

Julap* is a refreshing and wholesome drink, used much by country housewives. John Quincy,† the author of a dictionary of Physic, describes it as an extemporaneous form of medicine, made of simple and compound water sweetened, and serves for a vehicle to other forms not so convenient to take alone.

The usual mode of making it in the vicinage of Oxford is, by sweetening an infusion of mint with honey, and mixing a glass of wine or spirits with it.

The following is the Mint Julep of the Wenham Lake Company :

Mingle ice and sugar as described in the Recipe for Sherry Cobbler. Add a wine glass of brandy, half a wine glass of old rum,

* Julap is a Persian word, signifying a sweet potion.
† Died in 1728.

and two or three sprigs of mint. Stir the whole well together, and drink it through a straw.*

OXFORD PUNCH, OR CLASSICAL SHERBET.

> When e'en a bowl of punch we make,
> Four striking opposites we take;
> The strong, the small, the sharp, the sweet,
> Together mix'd, most kindly meet;
> And when they happily unite,
> The bowl is pregnant with delight.

The liquor called *Punch* has become so truly English, it is often supposed to be indigenous to this country, though its name at least is oriental. The Persian *punj*, or Sanscrit *pancha*, i. e. five,† is the etymon of its title, and denotes the number of ingredients

* The straws used are generally obtained from bonnet-makers, and are about eight inches long.

† See Fryer's Travels.

of which it is composed. Addison's *foxhunter*, who testified so much surprise when he found, that of the materials of which this " truly English " beverage was made, only the water belonged to England, would have been more astonished had his informant also told him, that it derived even its name from the East.

Various opinions are entertained respecting this compound drink. Some authors praise it as a cooling and refreshing beverage, when drank in moderation ; others condemn the use of it, as prejudicial to the brain and nervous system. Dr. Cheyne, a celebrated Scotch physician, author of " An Essay on Long Life and Health," and who by a system of diet and regimen reduced himself from the enormous weight of thirty-two stone to nearly one third, which enabled him to live to the age of seventy-two, insists, that there is but one wholesome ingredient in it, and that is the water. Dr. Willich, on the contrary, asserts, that if a proper quantity of acid be used in making Punch,

it is an excellent antiseptic, and well calcu-
lated to supply the place of wine in resisting
putrefaction, especially if drank cold with
plenty of sugar; it also promotes perspiration :
but if drank hot and immoderately, it creates
acidity in the stomach, weakens the nerves,
and gives rise to complaints of the breast.
He further states, that after a heavy meal it
is improper, as it may check digestion, and
injure the stomach.*

Rennie states, that he once heard a face-
tious physician at a public hospital prescribe
for a poor fellow sinking under the atrophy
of starvation, a bowl of *Rum Punch*. Mr
Wadd gives us a prescription—" Rum, aqua
dulci miscetur acetum, et fiet ex tali fœdere
nobile Punch." He also states, that Toddy,
or Punch without acid, when made for a day
or two before it is used, is a good and cheap
substitute for wine as a tonic, in convalescence
from typhus fever, &c.

*Fielding mentions a Clergyman who preferred Punch
to Wine for this orthodox reason, that the former was a
liquor no where spoken against in Scripture.

Recipe.

Extract the juice from the rind of three lemons, by rubbing loaf sugar on them. The peeling of two Seville oranges and two lemons, cut extremely thin. The juice of four Seville oranges and ten lemons. Six glasses of calves-feet jelly in a liquid state. The above to be put into a jug, and stirred well together. Pour two quarts of boiling water on the mixture, cover the jug closely, and place it near the fire for a quarter of an hour. Then strain the liquid through a sieve into a punch bowl or jug, sweeten it with a bottle of capillaire, and add half a pint of white wine, a pint of French brandy, a pint of jamaica rum, and a bottle of orange shrub; the mixture to be stirred as the spirits are poured in. If not sufficiently sweet, add loaf sugar gradually in small quantities, or a spoonful or two of capillaire. To be served up either hot or cold.* The Oxford Punch,

*Ignorant servants and waiters sometimes put oxalic acid into Punch to give it a flavour; such a practice cannot be too severely censured.

when made with half the quantity of spirituous liquors and placed in an ice tub for a short time, is a pleasant summer beverage.

In making this Punch, limes are sometimes used instead of lemons, but they are by no means so wholesome.†

NOYEAU PUNCH.

Mix three wine glasses of Noyeau with the Oxford Punch.

Noyeau is dangerous, when drank in any quantity, as it contains *hydrocyanic acid;* therefore more than the quantity specified ought not to be used.

SPICED PUNCH.

Boil a small quantity of each sort of spice in half a pint of water, until it is reduced one half; add it to the ingredients which compose the Oxford Punch, and grate a whole nutmeg into it. Spiced Punch, if bottled off

---

† Arbuthnot, in his work on ailments, says, "the West India dry gripes are occasioned by lime juice in Punch."

as soon as it is cold, with the spice in it, will keep good several days.

TEA PUNCH.

Green tea is the basis of this Punch; and although Tea Punch is seldom made in Oxford, it nevertheless has been much esteemed by those who have partaken of it. It is invariably drank hot. It is made precisely in the same way as the Oxford Punch, excepting that the jelly is omitted, and green tea supplies the place of water.

GIN PUNCH.

The same as Oxford Punch, only omit the rum, brandy, and shrub, and substitute two bottles of gin.

RED PUNCH.

Substitute port wine for white, and red currant jelly for calvesfeet jelly; in other respects the same as Oxford Punch. If drank in the summer, let it stand until it is cold, and then put it into a bucket of ice. Care must be taken that the ice water does not get into the jug which contains this Punch.

PUNCH ROYAL.

Extract the juice from the peeling of a lemon, by rubbing loaf sugar on it. Pour one pint of boiling water on it. Add the juice of six lemons, one pint of rum, and a pint of port wine. Sweeten it to your taste, and it is fit for use.

MILK PUNCH.

Warm two quarts of water and one of new milk, then mix them well together, and sweeten it with a sufficient quantity of loaf sugar. Rub a few knobs of loaf sugar on the peeling of a lemon; put them into a jug with the above, and pour into it gradually half a pint of lemon juice, stirring the mixture as it is poured in. Then add one quart of white brandy. Strain it through a flannel bag or a fine hair sieve. Bottle it off, and if placed in

c

a cool cellar it will keep ten days or a fortnight. Jellies are sometimes used in making this Punch, but they are not necessary, as the milk will sufficiently temper the acrimony of the lemon juice.

OXFORD MILK PUNCH.

Dissolve two pounds and a half of double refined sugar in one gallon of cold spring water; add to it a quarter of a pint of orange-flower water, the juice of twenty limes and eight pot oranges. Stir it well together; pour one quart of boiling milk into it, and then add three quarts of white brandy and three quarts of orange brandy shrub; strain it through a flannel bag or fine hair sieve. Take out what is wanted for present use, and bottle off the remainder.

NORFOLK MILK PUNCH.

Cut the peeling of six Seville oranges and six lemons extremely thin. Pound it in a stone mortar. Add thereto a pint of brandy,

and let it remain about six hours; then squeeze
the juice of six Seville oranges and eight
lemons into it. Stir it well, and pour into it
three more pints of brandy, three pints of rum,
and three quarts of water. Make two quarts
of skimmed milk boiling hot; grate a nutmeg
into it; mix it gradually with the other
ingredients; add a sufficient quantity of fine
loaf sugar to sweeten it, (about two pounds.)
Stir it till the sugar is dissolved. Let the
mixture stand twelve hours, then strain it
through a flannel bag till it is quite clear.
It is then fit for use. It has been said,
that if this Punch is bottled off and well
corked, it will keep in any climate, and
for any length of time.

The bottles it is put into must be
perfectly dry.

RESTORATIVE PUNCH, *vulgo*
STORATIVE.

Extract the juice from the peeling of one
Seville orange and one lemon; the juice of

six Seville oranges and six lemons, six glasses of calves-feet jelly in a liquid state, a sufficient quantity of loaf sugar, (about half a pound;) put the whole into a jug, pour on it one quart of boiling water; add four glasses of brandy, stir it well together, and it is fit for use.*

LEANDER PUNCH.

This drink was invented by Mr. Fellows, who was for many years an active member of the well-known "London Boat Club," from which it takes its name. The inventor caused the Punch to be introduced into the University by a friend at Ch. Ch.

Recipe.

Four glasses of whisky, (Irish if possible) two glasses of brandy, and the juice and peel of one large lemon. Add boiling water to make a quart, and if not enough, *ad libitum.*

* Many of the first statesmen of the present day (should they see this) will recognize it as the liquor invariably drank by them at College before they attended their debating parties.

Then boil a wine glass of good old ale, and put the froth into the punch with one tablespoonful of the ale ; sweeten to the taste and stir it. If it stands in a jug near the fire for half an hour it will be improved.

LEMON PUNCH TO KEEP.

Cut the rind off six lemons if large, eight if small, squeeze out the juice, put the rind and the juice together, and add one quart of white brandy. Let it remain closely covered for three or four days.

Let the juice of six or eight additional lemons be squeezed into two quarts of water, put into it a sufficient quantity of double refined sugar to sweeten the whole. Boil it well, and when quite cold, pour into it a bottle of sherry or madeira. Then mix it well with the lemon and brandy, and, if sufficiently sweet, strain it through a flannel bag into a small cask. At the expiration of three months bottle it off, and, if the bottles are well corked and kept in a cool place, it will be fit to drink in a month.

EGG PUNCH.

One quart of cold water, the juice of six lemons and six pot oranges, four glasses of calves-feet jelly in a liquid state; stir the whole well together; let it remain covered over for half an hour; then strain it through a hair sieve, and add to it a bottle of capillaire, two glasses of sherry, half a pint of brandy, and one bottle of orange shrub. Put some pulverised sugar and ten fresh-laid hens' eggs into a bowl, beat them well together, and gradually unite the two mixtures by keeping the eggs well stirred as it is poured in; then whip it with a whisk until a fine froth rises, and if sweet enough it is fit for immediate use.

This Punch should be drank as soon as it is made, for if kept for any length of time it will turn sour.

Omit the wine and spirits, and freeze the remainder, and a mould of ice may be obtained equal to any in use.

ALMOND PUNCH.

Extract the juice from the peeling of one lemon and one Seville orange by rubbing loaf sugar on them. The juice of six lemons and one Seville orange, one bottle of capillaire, and a quarter of a pound of loaf sugar. Put the whole into a jug, and when well mixed, pour upon it three pints of boiling water. Cover the jug close, and keep it near the fire a quarter of an hour. Then add three ounces of sweet and half an ounce of bitter almonds, blanched and pounded fine in a mortar, and gradually mixed with a bottle of white brandy. Stir it well, and if sufficiently sweet it may be used immediately.

SHRUB PUNCH.

To make the above into Shrub Punch of a superior flavour and quality to that in general use, merely leave out the eggs.

CHAMPAGNE PUNCH.

Pare two lemons very thin, and steep the peeling in one pint of rum, (or grate some lemon peel on a lump of sugar, and as the surface becomes yellow scrape it into the rum;) add a wine glass of sherry, half a pint of brandy, the juice of four lemons, a small quantity of syrup of capillaire, one quart of boiling water, sweeten it sufficiently with pounded sugar, and when those are assembled who intend to partake of it, pour into it a bottle of champagne.

PUNCH A LA ROMAINE.

Make one pint and a half of lemonade, beat to a froth the whites of four eggs, stir to this two ounces of pounded sugar, add half a quartern of rum, and the same quantity of brandy, with four glasses of green gooseberry or white currant wine.

This Punch is usually iced.

INN KEEPERS' PUNCH.

Dissolve about seven ounces of lump sugar in one pint of boiling water, add forty grains of citric acid, seven or eight drops of essence of lemon, and (when well mixed) half a pint of rum, a quarter of a pint of brandy, and a glass of sherry.

LEMONADE.

To convert Egg Punch into delicious Lemonade, leave out the wine, spirits, and oranges, and add the juice of four more lemons, and a proportionate quantity of sugar.

ORANGEADE.

The mixture may also be made into Orangeade by omitting the wine, spirits, and lemons, and squeezing into it the juice of twelve oranges in addition to those mentioned in the recipe for Egg Punch.

POSSET.

From fam'd Barbadoes, on the western main,
Fetch sugar, ounces four; fetch sack from Spain
A pint; and from the Eastern Indian coast
Nutmeg, the glory of our northern toast;
O'er flaming coals let them together heat,
Till the all-conquering sack dissolve the sweet;
O'er such another fire put eggs just ten,
New-born from tread of cock and rump of hen;
Stir them with steady hand and conscience pricking,
To see th' untimely end of ten fine chicken:
From shining shelf take down the brazen skellet,
A quart of milk from gentle cow will fill it;
When boiled and cold, put milk and sack to eggs;
Unite them firmly like the triple league,
And on the fire let them together dwell
Till miss sing twice—you must not kiss and tell:
Each lad and lass take up a silver spoon,
And fall on fiercely like a starved dragoon.

Sir Fleetwood Fletcher's Sack Posset.

———

POSSET, it seems, is a medicated drink of some antiquity; for among the numerous English authors who in some way or other speak of it, our immortal Bard Shakspeare has made one of his characters say, " We'll have a Posset at the latter end of a sea coal fire." And Sir John Suckling, who died in 1641, says in one of his poems, " In came the bridesmaids with the Posset." Dr. Johnson describes posset to be milk curdled with wine and other acids; we may therefore with propriety infer, that the White Wine Whey so common in Oxford, is the Milk Posset of our forefathers.

WHITE WINE WHEY, OR MILK POSSET.

Put one pint of milk into a saucepan, and when it boils pour into it one gill of white wine ; boil it till the curd becomes hard, then strain it through a fine sieve ; rub a few knobs of loaf sugar on the rind of a lemon, put them into the whey; grate a small quantity of nutmeg into it; sweeten it to your taste, and it is fit for use.

PEPPER POSSET.

The more to promote perspiration, whole pepper is sometimes boiled in the whey, but all-spice is far preferable.

A Pepper Posset was known to the learned and ingenious John Dryden, as will appear by the following lines written by him:—

> A sparing diet did her health assure;
> Or sick, a pepper posset was her cure.

CIDER POSSET.

Pound the peeling of a lemon in a mortar, pour on it one quart of fresh drawn cider; sweeten it with double-refined sugar, add one gill of brandy, and one quart of milk from the cow, stir it well together, strain it through a fine hair sieve or a flannel bag, then grate a nutmeg into it, and it is fit for use.

PERRY POSSET

is prepared in the same way, excepting that perry is used instead of cider.

There are other Possets, which have milk for their basis, in use in different parts of the country, such, for instance, as Treacle, Beer, and Orange Posset; but as they are seldom if ever made in Oxford, it is not necessary that anything further should be said of them.

The following have an affinity to, and possibly derived their origin from, Sir Fleetwood Fletcher's Sack Posset.

RUM BOOZE, OR EGG POSSET.*

The yolks of eight eggs well beaten up, with some refined sugar pulverised, and a grated nutmeg; extract the juice from the rind of a lemon by rubbing loaf sugar on it; put the sugar, a piece of cinnamon, and bottle of white wine, into a clean saucepan; when the wine boils take it off the fire; pour one glass of cold white wine into it, put it into a spouted jug, and pour it gradually among the yolks of eggs, &c., keeping them well stirred with a spoon as the wine is poured in: if not sweet enough add a small quantity of loaf sugar; then, pour the mixture as swift as possible from

* It is sometimes denominated *Egg Flip*

one vessel to the other until a fine white froth is obtained. Half a pint of rum is sometimes added, but it is then very intoxicating. Port wine is sometimes substituted for white, but it is not considered so palatable. This liquor should be drank when quite hot. If the wine is poured boiling hot among the eggs, the mixture will become curdled.

BEER FLIP.

Beer Flip is made in the same way and with the same materials as the preceding, excepting that one quart of strong home-brewed beer is substituted for the wine; a glass of gin is sometimes added, but it is better without it. This beverage is generally given to servants at Christmas, and other high festivals of our Church.

RUMFUSTIAN.

The yolks of twelve eggs, one quart of strong beer, one bottle of white wine, half a pint of gin, a grated nutmeg, the juice from the peeling of a lemon, a small quantity of cinnamon, and sufficient sugar to sweeten it; prepared precisely in the same way as Rum Booze.

Such is the intoxicating property of this liquor, that none but hard drinkers will venture to regale themselves with it a second time.

THE OXFORD GRACE CUP.

> The grace cup serv'd, the cloth away,
> Jove thought it time to shew his play.
> *Prior.*

The ancient Grace cup was a vessel proportioned to the number of the company assembled, which went round the table, the guests drinking out of the same cup one after another. Virgil describes something like it, when, speaking of the entertainment Queen Dido gave to Æneas, he says

Postquam prima quies epulis, menssæque remotæ ;
Crateras magnos statuunt, et vina coronant.
* * * * * * * * * *
Hic regina gravem gemmis auroque poposcit
Implevitique mero, pateram : * * * *
* * * * * * * * * * *
Primaque, libato, summo tenus attigit ore.
Tum Bitiæ dedit increpitans ; ille impiger hausit
Spumantem pateram, et pleno se proluit auro:
Post alii proceres.

It has been the custom from time immemorial, at the civic feasts in Oxford, for the Grace Cup to be introduced before the removal of the cloth, when the Mayor receives the Cup standing; his right and left hand guests also rise from their seats while he gives a toast, which, since the Reformation, has been "Church and King." The Cup is then handed round the table, no one presuming to apply his lips to it until two persons have risen from their seats. The origin of this custom is ascribed by our antiquaries to the practice of the Danes heretofore in England, who frequently used to stab or cut the throats of the natives while they were drinking, the persons standing being the sureties that the one holding the cup should come to no harm while partaking of it.

Recipe.

Extract the juice from the peeling of a lemon, and cut the remainder into thin slices; put it into a jug or bowl, and pour on it three half-pints of strong home brewed beer* and a bottle of mountain wine; grate a nutmeg into it; sweeten it to your taste; stir it till the sugar is dissolved, and then add three

---

* Home-brewed beer is here recommended, as some common brewers and publicans mix with their beer sulphuric acid, copperas, tobacco, capsicum, coculus Indicus, coriander seeds, grains of paradise, allum, and burnt sugar.

It is a well-known fact, thet at this period there are wandering from town to town persons who call themselves *"Brewers' Druggists,"* who offer for sale a composition

D

or four slices of bread toasted brown. Let it stand two hours, and then strain it off into the Grace Cup.

CIDER CUP, OR COLD TANKARD.

Cold Tankard has for a very long period been a favourite summer drink not only within the walls of the Colleges, but also at Taverns situated near the banks of the river, and which are much resorted to by the junior members of the University who

which in a short time will make weak beer strong, even to intoxication.

Coculus Indicus, the pulp of *Coculus suberosus*. Imported from the East Indies in considerable quantities, for the purpose, it is said, of giving beer and spirits an intoxicating quality at less expence than by genuine materials. The use of it is prohibited by law. *Rennie's Pharm.*

Grains of Paradise. In the slang of brewers' druggists termed G.P. The seeds of the *Amomum grana Paradisi.* They are seldom used in medicine, but are extensively employed to conceal adulterations by giving false strength to spirits, wine, beer, and vinegar. *Ibid.*

are fond of aquatic excursions. Many are
the sonnets and songs which have been
made upon the fair waiting women who
almost invariably prepare this cooling and
wholesome beverage. The following specimen,
written some years since, probably will not
prove unacceptable to the reader.

Say—lives far or near a damsel so fair,
So cheerful, so blithe, or so merry?
    On earth I can't find
    A nymph half so kind
As Doris, the Maid of the Ferry.

My rivals may boast, and coxcombs may toast
Her in old port, madeira, or sherry;
    To them I can prove,
    They'll ne'er gain the love
Of Doris, the Maid of the Ferry.

She looks up the oars, and the old tavern scores,
And now and then cleans out a wherry;
    The sails she can mend,
    And the parlour attend,
For obliging's the Maid of the Ferry.

She serves at the bar, and excels all by far
In making Cold Tankard of perry;
　　How sweet then at eve,
　　With her leave to receive
A kiss from the Maid of the Ferry.

Both early and late her apparel is neat,
Yet for finery she cares not a berry;
　　She's comely and gay,
　　And now I'll away
To Doris, the Maid of the Ferry.

Recipe.

Extract the juice from the peeling of one lemon, by rubbing loaf sugar on it; cut two lemons into thin slices; the rind of one lemon cut thin, a quarter of a pound of loaf sugar, and half a pint of brandy.　Put the whole into a large jug, mix it well together, and pour one quart of cold spring water upon it. Grate a nutmeg into it, add one pint of white wine and a bottle of cider, sweeten it to your taste with capillaire or sugar, put a hand-

ful of balm and the same quantity of borage*
in flower (*borago officinalis*) into it, stalk
downwards. Then put the jug containing
this liquor into a tub of ice, and when it
has remained there one hour it is fit for
use. The balm and borage should be fresh
gathered.

PERRY CUP.

Merely substitute perry for cider.

* " The sprigs of borage in wine are of known virtue, to
revive the hypochondriac, and cheer the hard student."
Evelyn's Acetaria, p. 18. " Borage is one of the four
cordial flowers; it comforts the heart, cheers melancholy,
and revives the fainting spirits." *Salmon's Household
Companion*, London, 1710. " Borage has the credit of
being a great cordial; throwing it into cold wine is better
than all the medicinal preparations." *Sir John Hill, M.D.*

" The leaves, flowers, and seeds of borage, all or any of
them, are good to expel pensiveness and melancholy."
The English Physician.

" Balm is very good to help digestion and open obstruc-
tions of the brain, and hath so much purging quality in
it, as to expel those melancholy vapours from the spirits
and blood which are in the heart and arteries, although
it cannot do so in other parts of the body." *Ibid.*

BEER CUP.

One quart of strong beer instead of cider or perry. The other ingredients the same as in Cider Cup.

RED CUP.

Use one pint of port wine instead of white; sometimes two glasses of red currant jelly are added. In other respects the same as Cider Cup, excepting that warm water is used to dissolve the jelly.

THE WASSAIL BOWL, OR SWIG.

"Sir, quod he, Watsayll, for never days of your lyf ne dronk ye of such a cuppe." *Ancient MS.*

The Wassail Bowl, or Swig, as it is termed at Jesus College in this University, is of considerable antiquity, and up to this time is a great favorite with the sons of Cambria; so much so, indeed, that a party seldom dines or sups in that College without its forming

a part of their entertainment.*　On the festival
of St. David, Cambria's tutelary Saint, an
immense silver gilt bowl, containing ten
gallons, and which was presented to Jesus
College by Sir Watkin W. Wynne in 1732,
is filled with Swig, and handed round to
those who are invited on that occasion to
sit at their festive and hospitable board.
The following is the method of manufacturing
it at that College.

Recipe.

Put into a bowl half a pound of Lisbon
sugar; pour on it one pint of warm beer;
grate a nutmeg and some ginger into it;
add four glasses of sherry and five additional
pints of beer; stir it well; sweeten it to
your taste: let it stand covered up two or
three hours, then put three or four slices of
bread cut thin and toasted brown into it,
and it is fit for use.　Sometimes a couple or

* Swig was formerly almost exclusively confined to
Jesus College; it is now, however, a great favourite
throughout the University.

three slices of lemon, and a few lumps of loaf sugar rubbed on the peeling of a lemon, are introduced.

Bottle this mixture, and in a few days it may be drank in a state of effervescence.

The Wassail Bowl, or Wassail Cup, was formerly prepared in nearly the same way as at present, excepting that roasted apples, or crab apples, were introduced instead of toasted bread. And up to the present period in some parts of the kingdom, there are persons who keep up the ancient custom of regailing their friends and neighbours on Christmas-eve and Twelfth-eve with a Wassail Bowl, with roasted apples floating in it, and which is generally ushered in with great ceremony. Shakspeare alludes to the Wassail Bowl when he says, in his Midsummer Night's Dream,

> Sometimes lurk I in a gossip's bowl,
> In very likeness of a roasted crab,
> And when she drinks, against her lips I bob,
> And on her wither'd dewlap pour the ale.

BROWN BETTY.

Brown Betty does not differ materially from the preceding; it is said to have derived its name from one of the *fair sex*, ycleped a bedmaker, who invariably recommended the mixture so named as a never failing panacea.

Recipe.

Dissolve a quarter of a pound of brown sugar in one pint of water, slice a lemon into it, let it stand a quarter of an hour, then add a small quantity of pulverised cloves and cinnamon, half a pint of brandy, and one quart of good strong ale; stir it well together, put a couple of slices of toasted bread into it, grate some nutmeg and ginger on the toast, and it is fit for use. Ice it well and it will prove a good summer, warm it and it will become a pleasant winter, beverage. It is drank chiefly at dinner.

LAMBS WOOL.

Next crowne the bowle full
With gentle Lambs wooll,
    Adde sugar, nutmeg, and ginger,
With store of ale too,
And thus ye must doe
      To make the Wassaile a swinger.

Herrick's Twelfth Night, or King and Queen.

Lambs Wool is merely a variety of the Wassail Bowl, and although not common in Oxford, is a great favourite in some parts of England. The following is the origin of the term Lambs Wool, as applied to this particular beverage. Formerly the first day of November was dedicated to the Angel presiding over fruits, seeds, &c., and was therefore named *La mas ubal*, that is, The day of the apple fruit, and being pronounced *lamasool*, our country people have corrupted it to Lambs Wool.*

* See Col. Vallancy, Collect. de Reb. Hibern. iii. 441.

Lambs Wool was anciently often met with in Ireland,* but is now rarely heard of in that country, having been entirely super-seded by the more intoxicating liquor called Whiskey.

Recipe.

Mix the pulp of half a dozen roasted apples with some raw sugar, a grated nut-meg, and a small quantity of ginger. Add one quart of strong ale made moderately warm. Stir the whole well together, and, if sweet enough, it is fit for use.

This mixture is sometimes served up in bowl, with sweet cakes floating in it.

* Brand's Popul. Antiq. i. 821.

BRASENOSE ALE.

Hic dies, anno redeunte festus.
Corticem adstrictum pice dimovebit
Amphorae.

Horat. lib. iii. od. 8.

When the year
Revolving bids this festal morn appear,
We'll pierce a cask with mellow juice replete.
Francis.

From the Foundation of Brasenose College
to the present time a custom has prevailed,
of introducing into the refectory on Shrove
Tuesday, immediately after dinner, what is
denominated Brasenose Ale, but which in
fact is a species of Lambs Wool.

Verses in praise of Brasenose Ale are an-
nually written by one of the Undergraduates
and a copy of them sent to every resident
member of the College.

The following Stanzas are extracted from
a copy of recent date.

Shall all our singing now be o'er,
Since Christmas carols fail?
No! let us shout one stanza more
In praise of Brasenose Ale!

A fig for Horace and his juice,
Falernian and Massic;
Far better drink can we produce,
Though 'tis not quite so Classic.

Not all the liquors Rome e'er had
Can beat our matchless Beer;
Apicius' self had gone stark mad,
To taste such noble cheer.

Brasenose Verses are not always confined
to the mere praise of the Beer, for sometimes
a particular circumstance or event which
may have happened during the past year is
alluded to, as will be seen by the following
lines.

See where yon goblet beaming
Invites the wistful eye!
Whose smile luxuriant gleaming
Proclaims a fragrance nigh!

While gladsome spirits thronging round
  To taste its richness press;
And fair the scene, and loud the sound
  Of mirth and happiness !

Bright antidote of sorrow !
  Some kind enlivening ray
From thee we fain would borrow,
  To warm our grateful lay:
For oft I ween thy kindling glance
  The drooping heart hath cheered :
Poured round the soul a joyous trance,
  And visions gay upreared.

Full many a day of gladness
  Hath hailed the welcome cheer;
Full many a thought of sadness
  Hath fled, transported, here.
And still, through years of fleeting change,
  Each passing youthful train,
Ere it might tempt the wide world's range,
  Hath passed the cup to drain.

The sky that glows above us
  Remains unchanged the same:
But will the friends that love us
  Preserve a changeless flame ?

Forgetfulness, that chilling spell,
  Can freeze the ardent breast ;
And those we thought had loved us well,
  Will scorn us when distressed.

While warm affection glowing
  Bids mean suspicion fly,
Our youthful hearts bestowing
  On most that hover nigh—
When outward promise seems sincere,
  And lasting all our joy—
Yet cherished hope, and feelings dear
  Unkindness may destroy.

The word of coldness spoken
  Inflicts a bitter smart ;
The tie of friendship broken
  Torments the aching heart :
But sadder far the hopeless pain,
  When death's remorseless hand
Hath all untimely snapped in twain
  Affection's golden band.

But, though our friends forget us,
  Let one kind thought restore
Their names, who once have met us
  But ne'er shall meet us more.

And if, perchance, by memory's light
  Departed friends we view,
Oh ! let that memory still be bright,
  And may our hearts be true !

When last the cup was flowing,
  One sat within our Hall,
Whose eye with kindness glowing
  Inspire the festival.*
But now that bright and honoured head
  Rests in the darkling tomb;
And ours it is to mourn the dead
  In unavailing gloom.

Forgive the Muse, if, erring,
  He drop a plaintful word :
If, thoughts of sorrow stirring,
  He strike too harsh a chord.
We would not mar the festive scene,
  Nor give a wanton pain ;
And, though her strains have saddening been,
  She bids you smile again.

---

  * This passage alludes to the demise of an Under-graduate, who at the preceding meeting had, by his wit and humour, contributed much to the hilarity of his fellow-students.

In banquet-hall 'tis meetest
  To raise the echoing laugh:
In jocund hour 'tis sweetest
  The bowl's deep flood to quaff.
Aye ! let your mirth be loud and long !
  Let voice and heart be free !
And 'midst the din of shout and song
  Let all feast merrily !

Go forth, my sons, to glory !
  Go climb the steeps of fame !
Go ! and in future story
  Enrol your shining name !
May no dark cloud obscure your sky;
  No fear your soul dismay ;
Nor keener sorrow dim your eye
  Than claims the tear to day !

Recipe.

Three quarts of ale, sweetened with refined sugar finely pulverised, and served
up in a bowl with six roasted apples floating
in it.

————

E

METHEGLIN.

Non Vitis, sed Apis succum tibi mitto bibendum,
Quem legimus Bardos olim potasse Britannos.
Qualibet in bacca Vitis Megera latescit,
Qualibet in gutta Mellis Aglaia nitet.

The juice of Bees, not Bacchus, here behold,
Which British Bards were wont to quaff of old ;
The berries of the grape with Furies swell,
But in the honeycomb the Graces dwell.

Howell.

Metheglin is probably derived from the Welch Meodyglyn,* a medical drink, and was once the natural beverage of a great part of this country, and according to some authors is the Hydromel† of the ancients. Howell,‡ in one of his familiar letters, on

* Meddyglyn. *Minshew.*

† In fevers, the ailments prescribed by Hippocrates were ptisans and cream of barley, *hydromel*, that is, honey and water, where there was no tendency to delirium.

Arbuthnot.

‡ James Howell, Clerk of the Privy Council in 1640, and sometimes Fellow of Jesus College in this University.

presenting a friend with a bottle of Metheglin, thus speaks of it; "Neither Sir John
"Barleycorn or Bacchus had anything to do
"with it, but it is the pure juice of the bee,
"the laborious bee, and the king of insects;
"the Druids and old British Bards were wont
"to take a carouse hereof before they entered
"into their speculations, But this drink always
"carries a kind of state with it, for it must be
"attended with a brown toast; nor will it admit
"but of one good draught, and that in the
"morning; if more, it will keep a *humming* in
"the head, and so speak too much of the house
"it comes from, I mean, the hive."

Indeed almost every other author who has
written on the subject affirms, that before
the introduction of Agriculture into this
island, honey diluted with water (i. e. Metheglin) was the only strong drink known
to, and was a great favorite among, the
Ancient Britons.

Metheglin is usually divided into the
Simple and the Vinous. Simple Metheglin

is that which has not been fermented, and the Vinous is that which has obtained a spirit by fermentation.

VINOUS METHEGLIN.

Take as much new honey separated from the comb, which, when well mixed with water, will be of such a consistency as to bear an egg; boil this liquor for one hour; let it stand covered up till the next morning, and if it is then quite cold, put it into a cask. To every fifteen gallons add pulverized ginger, mace, cinnamon, and cloves, of each an ounce. To promote fermentation, put into the bunghole two table-spoonfuls of yeast. When it has done working stop it up, and in a month or six weeks it will be in a fit state to be drawn off into bottles.

Or put twenty-eight pounds of honey into a nine-gallon cask with as much boiling water as will fill it, and fermenting it with yeast. Or boil the honey with the water, to which a little hops or ginger may be added, ferment, and bottle for use.

MEAD AND BRAGGON, OR BRAGGET,

Do not differ materially from Metheglin; they are indeed varieties of the same. Howell says, "they differ in strength according to "the three degrees of comparison, Metheglin "being strong in the superlative, and if "taken immoderately doth stupify more than "any other liquor."

The following are the methods of preparing them.

Mix the whites of six eggs with twelve gallons of spring water; add twenty pounds of the best virgin honey and the peeling of three lemons; boil it an hour, and then put into it some rosemary,* cloves, mace, and ginger; when it is quite cold, add a spoonful or two of yeast, tun it, and when it has done working, stop it up close. In a few months bottle it off, and deposit it in a cellar of cool temperature.

* The best honey known is that of Narbonne in France, where rosemary abounds, it having a very strong flavor of that plant.

Some prefer it without the spices, others without lemons.

To each gallon of water add four pounds of the whitest, purest, and best tasted honey, and the peeling of two lemons; boil it half an hour. Scum it when cold. Put it into a cask, add some yeast to it; when it has done fermenting, stop the cask up close, and at the expiration of eight months bottle off.

If this liquor is properly kept, the taste of the honey will go off, and it will resemble Tokay both in strength and flavour.

The following Cups are added to the original work.

CLARET CUP.

Two bottles of claret, two bottles of soda water, one wine glass of brandy, half a wine glass of curacoa, the peel of one lemon (very thin), sweetened with capillaire or powdered sugar according to taste, Wenham Lake Ice, three or four sprigs of borage.

Claret Cup should be made an hour previous to the time wanted. Mix the claret, brandy, curacoa, capillaire, and lemon peel together, then add the soda water, borage, and Wenham Lake ice before useing it.

CHAMPAGNE CUP.

Two bottles of Champagne, two bottles of soda water, half a wine glass of brandy, half a wine glass of curacoa, the peel of one lemon (very thin), Whenham Lake ice, one table-spoonful of powdered sugar.

Mix all the ingredients together except the ice, which add when serving.

MOSELLE CUP.

Two bottles of sparkling Moselle, two bottles of soda water, half a wine glass of brandy, half a wine glass of curacoa, the peel of one lemon (peeled very thin), sweeten with capillaire to taste, Wenham Lake ice.

Mix all the above ingredients together then add the ice when serving.

THE END.

Classic Cocktail Resource Guide

Some ingredients found in vintage cocktail guides are unavailable or hard to come by today. However, the creation of historically accurate cocktails is a growing hobby, and with a bit of Internet research, you will find recipes for bitters and syrups online, as well as manufacturers that are developing new product lines for the classic cocktail enthusiast.

Vendors

A short selection of online vendors selling bitters, mixers, syrups, wine, liqueurs, and spirits. This list is by no means complete but is a good place to start your search.

BevMo!
www.bevmo.com

Binny's Beverage Depot
www.binnys.com

The Bitter Truth
www.the-bitter-truth.com

Cocktail Kingdom
www.cocktailkingdom.com

Fee Brothers
www.feebrothers.com

Hi-Time Wine Cellars
www.hitimewine.net

Internet Wines and Spirits
www.internetwines.com

The Jug Shop
www.thejugshop.com

Monin Gourmet Flavorings
www.moninstore.com

The Whiskey Exchange
www.thewhiskyexchange.com

General Interest

These sites provide background information on individual ingredients, suggestions for substitutes, current commercial availability, and recipes.

The Chanticleer Society
A Worldwide Organization of Cocktail Enthusiasts
www.chanticleersociety.org

Drink Boy
Adventures in Cocktails
www.drinkboy.com

The Internet Cocktail Database Ingredients Search
www.cocktaildb.com/ingr_search

Museum of the American Cocktail
www.museumoftheamericancocktail.org

WebTender Wiki
www.wiki.webtender.com

Coming Soon from
Classic Cocktail Guides
and Retro Bartender Books

Home Made Beverages

The Manufacture of Non-Alcoholic and
Alcoholic Drinks in the Household, Including
Recipes for Essences, Extracts, and Syrups

A Pre-Prohibition Cocktail Book

Albert Hopkins

Cocktails: How to Make Them

An 1898 Bartender's Guide

Livermore & Knight

ISBN: 978-1-880954-35-5

Classic Cocktail Guides
and Retro Bartender Books

Jack's Manual of Recipes for Fancy Mixed Drinks and How to Serve Them

A Pre-Prohibition Cocktail Book

J. A. Grohusko

ISBN: 978-1-880954-28-7

Classic Cocktail Guides
and Retro Bartender Books

Stuart's Fancy Drinks and How to Mix Them

Containing Clear and Practical Directions for
Mixing All Kinds of Cocktails, Sours, Egg Nog,
Sherry Cobblers, Coolers, Absinthe, Crustas,
Fizzes, Flips, Juleps, Fixes, Punches, Lemonades,
Pousse Cafes, Invalids' Drinks, Etc. Etc.

Thomas Stuart

ISBN: 978-1-880954-34-8

Classic Cocktail Guides
and Retro Bartender Books

What to Drink

Non~Alcoholic Drinks and Cocktails
Served During Prohibition

Bertha E. L. Stockbridge

ISBN: 978-1-880954-36-2

Classic Cocktail Guides
and Retro Bartender Books

Nineteenth-Century Cocktail Creations

How to Mix Drinks: A Bar Keeper's Handbook

George Winter

ISBN: 978-1-880954-30-0